Quick HANGEUL

Quick Hangeul
How to Read Korean Alphabet in One Hour!

Written by Heechul Cho
Publisher Kyudo Chung
Published by Darakwon

First Published 2025. 3. 20

Editorial Planner Hyukju Kwon, Taekwang Kim
Editor Huchun Lee, Hyoeun Kim, Soyoung Park

Designed by SINGTA Design
Image iclickart, shutterstock

DARAKWON

Darakwon Bldg., 211 Munbal-ro, Paju-si, Gyeonggi-do, Republic of Korea 10881
Tel : 02-736-2031
Fax : 02-732-2037
(Marketing Dept. ext.:250~252, Editorial Dept. ext.: 291~296)

http://www.darakwon.co.kr
http://www.darakwonusa.com

Visit the Darakwon homepage to learn about our other publications and promotions and to download the contents in MP3 format.

한글 빨리 마스터 하기!

Quick HANGEUL

Master **Korean Alphabet**
Through Visual Examples

Written by **Heechul Cho**

How to Read Korean Alphabet in ONE HOUR!

DARAKWON

Preface

The Korean alphabet, Hangeul, is the first step to learning the Korean language. The challenge of learning Hangeul is in the number of characters and it's unique trait, which allows new characters to be created by combining existing characters. Hence, learning Hangeul is more difficult than people commonly think.

I have been teaching Korean to university students and the general public in Japan for quite some time, and I understand very well how difficult it is to learn Hangeul. There are countless cases where people cannot read Korean correctly even after studying Hangeul for months, so I developed a new way to memorize Hangeul with images.

Many Westerners who learn Korean perceive Hangeul as similar to pictographs. The mnemonic proposed in this book is based on the concept of Hangeul's pictorial appearance. This book is the English version of "A Textbook to Read Hangeul in One Hour," which was published in Japan in 2011 and has sold over 800,000 copies (including similar books) to date, receiving overwhelming support from readers.

Naturally, this book is designed to make it easy for native English speakers to learn Hangeul. I hope that everyone who picks up this book will have fun and learn Hangeul easily.

I would like to thank Dain Kim for giving me many ideas and for publishing this book, Jihye Kim and Lisandra Moor for checking the English expressions, and Huchun Lee of Publisher Darakwon Publishing.

Heechul Cho

A comprehensive introduction to the Korean Alphabet!

This book focuses on learning Hangeul so you can read and write with confidence!

Vowels & Consonants

You can learn shapes and sounds of consonants and vowels. Try writing the hangeul in the correct stroke order and practice the pronunciation. And you'll discover a wide vocabulary through the letters you've learned.

Visual Examples

A variety of visual examples are provided to show how each letter is used. You'll also learn useful Korean words.

Audio files

You can learn the correct pronunciation of each word by listening to native Korean speakers. As you listen and read multiple times, you'll naturally become familiar with Korean pronunciation.

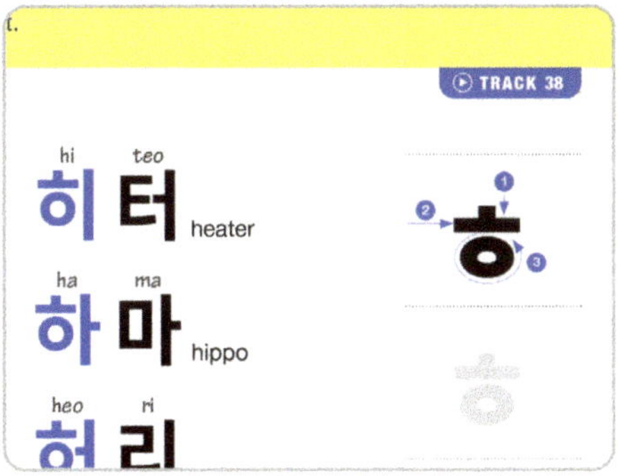

FREE
Audio files
www.darakwonusa.com

Review

Each chapter includes writing practice to review words you've learned.

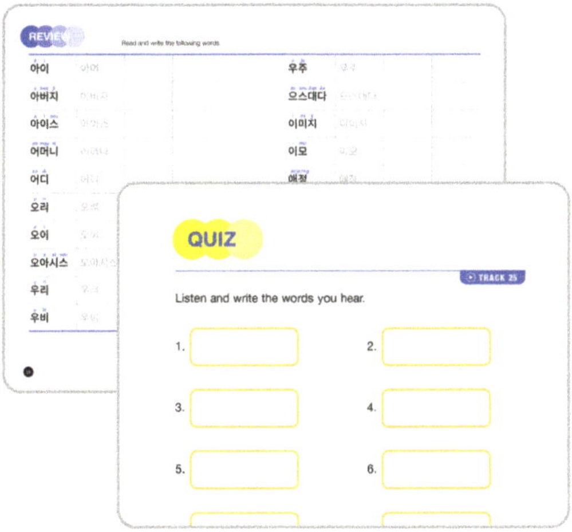

Appendix

The [Appendix] includes various styles of Hangeul letters, helping you become familiar with their characteristics. Additionally, learners can practice reading and writing basic Korean expressions.

Table of Contents

Preface 4

How to use this book 6

PART 1
Korean Vowels

1 The Different Types of Simple Vowels(eight vowels) 14

아 어 오 우 으 이 애 에

2 The "Y" Group Vowels 26

야 여 요 유 얘 예

3 The "W" Group Vowels 42

와 왜 외 워 웨 위

4 The Diphthongs Vowel 58

의

PART 2
Korean Consonants

1 The Composition of Korean Consonants 64

2 The Pronunciation of Consonants

1. Normal Sound 69

ㄱ ㄴ ㄷ ㄹ ㅁ ㅂ ㅅ ㅇ ㅈ

2. Aspirated sound 89

ㅋ ㅌ ㅍ ㅎ ㅊ

3. Tense sound 101

ㄲ ㄸ ㅃ ㅆ ㅉ

4. 'Batchim', final consonant ① 113

5. 'Batchim', final consonant ② double batchim 124

APPENDIX

1. Various fonts in Hangeul 134

2. Korean basic expression 138

PART 1

Korean Vowels

Vowels of Hangeul are created by combining '·, ㅡ, ㅣ.' The combination of these three characters creates a multiplicity of vowels.

For example, adding '·' to the right of 'ㅣ' makes 'ㅏ[a]' and adding '·' on top of 'ㅡ[eu]' makes 'ㅗ[o].'

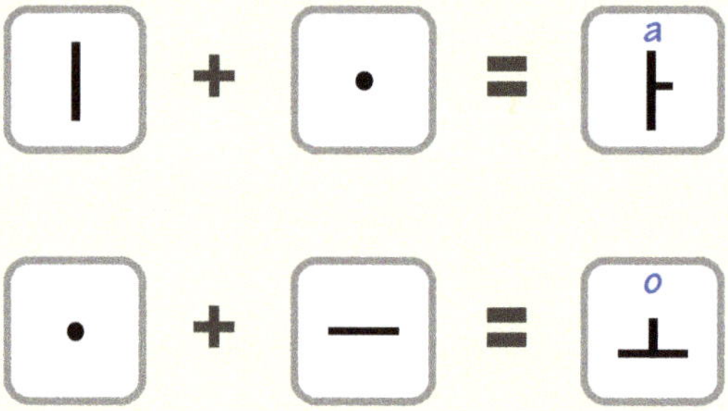

Adding '·' to the left of 'ㅣ' makes 'ㅓ[eo]' and adding '·' under 'ㅡ' makes 'ㅜ[u].'

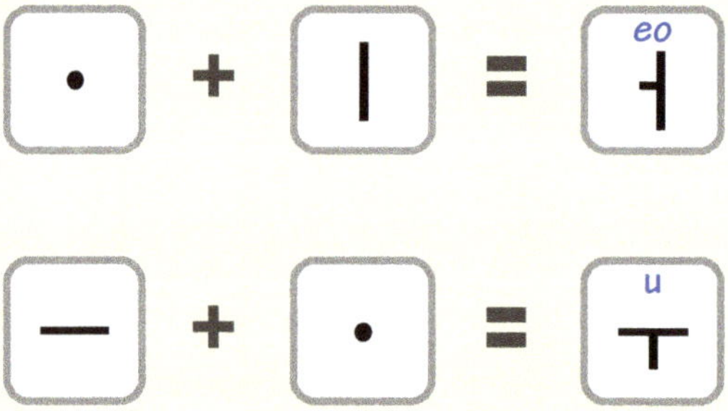

Adding another '·' to the above-mentioned vowels gives us 'ㅑ[ya]/ㅛ[yo]' and 'ㅕ[yeo]/ㅠ[yu],' respectively.

ㅏ (a) + · = ㅑ (ya)

ㅗ (o) + · = ㅛ (yo)

ㅓ (eo) + · = ㅕ (yeo)

ㅜ (u) + · = ㅠ (yu)

The Korean vowels that can be made with this combination are as follows. The consonant "ㅇ" will act as a silent placeholder.

아	야	어	여	오			요	우			유	으	이
애	얘	에	예	와	왜	외		워	웨	위		의	

1

The Different Types of Simple Vowels (eight vowels)

Korean vowels are consisted of 10 simple vowels and 11 complex vowels. Based on pronunciation, however, there is a total of 8 simple vowels in addition to the 13 complex vowels created by synthesizing the aforementioned simple vowels.

Simple vowels refer to a set of vowels that do not require a change the position of the tongue or the shape of the lips — otherwise known as a speaker's articulators. On the contrary, complex vowels are those by which the position of the tongue or the shape of the lips changes upon pronunciation.

From now on, we will examine the simple vowels.

a 아	eo 어	o 오	u 우
eu 으	i 이	ae 애	e 에

The followings are the eight simple vowels.

TRACK 01

a

아

eo

어

o

오

u

우

eu

으

i

이

ae

애

e

에

Let's learn about the sounds and shapes of the vowels, and the words they are used in.

ㅏ(아) sounds like a in father

f ㅏ ther

ㅏ = 아 → a

▶ TRACK 02

아

a	i	
아	이	child
a	beo	ji
아	버	지 father
a	i	seu
아	이	스 ice

① ② ㅏ

ㅏ

ㅏ

Find the letters **아** in the images below.

아메리카노

아빠

아이스크림

ㅓ(어) sounds like *eo* in fath*er*

fath ㅓ r

ㅓ = 어 → eo

TRACK 03

eo	meo	ni	
어	머	니	mother

eo	bu	
어	부	fisherman

eo	di	
어	디	where

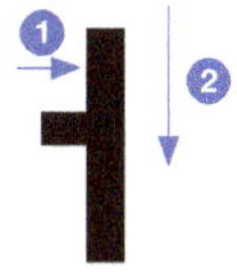

Find the letters **어** in the images below.

어워드

아이디어

어린이날

ㅗ(오) sounds like o in door

d ㅗ r

ㅗ = 오 → o

▶ TRACK 04

o	ri		
오	리		

duck

o	i
오	이

cucumber

o	a	si	seu
오	아	시	스

oasis

① ㅗ ②

Find the letters 오 in the images below.

오늘

오래오래

오리

ㅜ(우) sounds like u in food

f ㅜ d

ㅜ = 우 → u

TRACK 05

우 (u) 리 (ri) we

우 (u) 비 (bi) raincoat

우 (u) 주 (ju) universe

ㅜ

Find the letters 우 in the images below.

우리 한우

우유

우동

ㅡ(으) sounds like eu in sky

s ㅡ ky

ㅡ = 으 → eu

ㅡ(으) sounds like between the letter “s” and “ky” in the word “sky.” There is no equivalent vowel in the English language. When you pronounce ‘으’, pull your lips back and make sure your lips aren’t protruding outward.

TRACK 06

eu seu dae da
으스대다
show off

eu ri eu ri ha da
으리으리하다
magnificent

1
ㅡ

Find the letters 으 in the images below.

으뜸

으쓱

으라차차

ㅣ(이) sounds like i in kiss

k ㅣ ss

ㅣ = 이 → i

TRACK 07

이

i	ri		
이	리		wolf
i	mi	ji	
이	미	지	image
i	mo		
이	모		aunt

ㅣ ①

Find the letters **이** in the images below.

마이, 라이프

이사

이천

ㅐ (애) sounds like ae in apple

애pple

ㅐ = 애 → ae

TRACK 08

ae 애	jeong 정	love
ae 애	gyo 교	charms
ae 애	su 수	sorrow

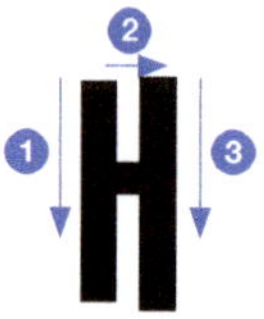

ㅐ

ㅐ

Find the letters **애** in the images below.

연애

애견

애그플레이션

ㅔ(에) sounds like e in error

에rror

ㅔ = 에 → e

TRACK 09

에

e	eo	keon	
에	어	컨	airconditioner
e	neo	ji	
에	너	지	energy
e	i	seu	
에	이	스	ace

Find the letters **에** in the images below.

무이네에서

에너지

크리에이터

REVIEW

Read and write the following words.

a i 아이	아이		
a beo ji 아버지	아버지		
a i seu 아이스	아이스		
eo meo ni 어머니	어머니		
eo di 어디	어디		
o ri 오리	오리		
o i 오이	오이		
o a si seu 오아시스	오아시스		
u ri 우리	우리		
u bi 우비	우비		

u ju 우주	우주		
eu seu dae da 으스대다	으스대다		
i mi ji 이미지	이미지		
i mo 이모	이모		
ae jeong 애정	애정		
ae gyo 애교	애교		
ae su 애수	애수		
e eo keon 에어컨	에어컨		
e neo ji 에너지	에너지		
e i seu 에이스	에이스		

2 The "Y" Group Vowels

There is a total of 6 "Y" group vowels. They are created by adding short horizontal or vertical stroke to the 6 vowels — **아**[a], **어**[eo], **오**[o], **우**[u], **애**[ae], **에**[e] — with the exception of '**으/이**.'

Combination	Example
ㅏ (a) + • = ㅑ (ya)	야 갸 냐 먀 샤
ㅓ (eo) + • = ㅕ (yeo)	여 겨 녀 며 셔
ㅗ (o) + • = ㅛ (yo)	요 교 뇨 묘 쇼
ㅜ (u) + • = ㅠ (yu)	유 규 뉴 뮤 슈
ㅐ (ae) + • = ㅒ (yae)	얘 걔 쟤
ㅔ (e) + • = ㅖ (ye)	예 계 례 폐 혜

TRACK 10

ya
야

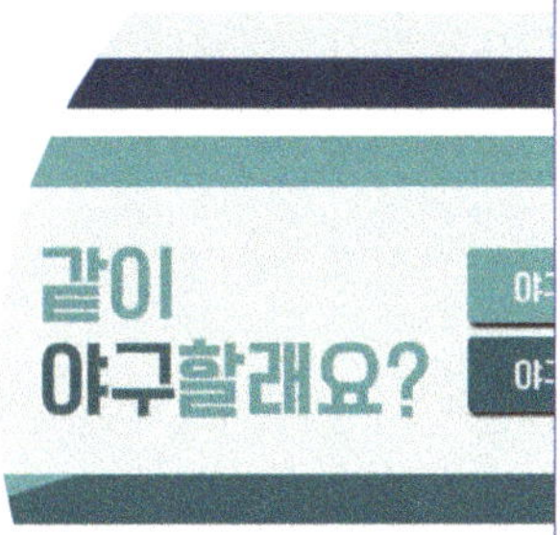

yeo
여

yo
요

yu
유

yae
얘

ye
예

▸ The consonant ㅇ will act as a silent placeholder.

ㅑ (야) sounds like ya in shout

sh ㅑ ut

ya		a
ㅑ	from	ㅏ

TRACK 11

ya
ㅑ

ㅇ	+	ya ㅑ	=	ya 야
g ㄱ	+	ya ㅑ	=	gya 갸
n ㄴ	+	ya ㅑ	=	nya 냐
m ㅁ	+	ya ㅑ	=	mya 먀
s ㅅ	+	ya ㅑ	=	sya 샤

ㅑ

ya gu
야구 baseball

sya weo
샤워 shower

e seu pa nya
에스파냐 Espana

Find the letters ‘consonant + ㅑ’ in the images below.

심야

샤워

에스파냐

ㅕ (여) sounds like yeo in yummy

여 mmy

yeo		eo
ㅕ	from	ㅓ

TRACK 12

yeo
ㅕ

ㅇ	+	ㅕ (yeo)	=	여 (yeo)
ㄱ (g)	+	ㅕ (yeo)	=	겨 (gyeo)
ㄴ (n)	+	ㅕ (yeo)	=	녀 (nyeo)
ㅁ (m)	+	ㅕ (yeo)	=	며 (myeo)
ㅅ (s)	+	ㅕ (yeo)	=	셔 (syeo)

ㅕ

yeo ja
여자 woman

syeo teo
셔터 shutter

myeo neu ri
며느리 daughter-in-law

ㅕ ㅕ ㅕ

Find the letters 'consonant + ㅕ' in the images below.

겨울

해녀

여름

ㅛ(요) sounds like yo in yoga

요 ga

yo
ㅛ
from
o
ㅗ

TRACK 13

yo
ㅛ

ㅇ	+	yo ㅛ	=	yo 요
g ㄱ	+	yo ㅛ	=	gyo 교
n ㄴ	+	yo ㅛ	=	nyo 뇨
m ㅁ	+	yo ㅛ	=	myo 묘
s ㅅ	+	yo ㅛ	=	syo 쇼

ㅛ

yo ri
요리 cooking

myo sa
묘사 description

syo teu ke i keu
쇼트케이크 shortcake

ㅛ ㅛ ㅛ

Find the letters ‘consonant + ㅛ’ in the images below.

쇼핑

교실

애묘

ㅠ(유) sounds like yu in you

유

yu ㅠ	from	u ㅜ

TRACK 14

yu
ㅠ

ㅇ	+	yu ㅠ	=	yu 유
g ㄱ	+	yu ㅠ	=	gyu 규
n ㄴ	+	yu ㅠ	=	nyu 뉴
m ㅁ	+	yu ㅠ	=	myu 뮤
s ㅅ	+	yu ㅠ	=	syu 슈

ㅠ

yu ri
유리 glass

gyu mo
규모 scale

nyu seu
뉴스 news

ㅠ ①②③ ㅠ ㅠ

Find the letters 'consonant + ㅠ' in the images below.

뉴욕

슈

유기농

ㅒ (얘) sounds like yea in yeah

얘

yae ㅒ	from	ae ㅐ

TRACK 15

yae ㅒ

ㅇ	+	yae ㅒ	=	yae 얘
g ㄱ	+	yae ㅒ	=	gyae 걔
s ㅅ	+	yae ㅒ	=	syae 섀
j ㅈ	+	yae ㅒ	=	jyae 쟤

yae gi
얘 기 story

syae do
섀 도 shadow

ha yae yo
하 얘 요 white

Find the letters 'consonant + ㅒ' in the images below.

아이섀도

얘들

하얘요

ㅖ (예) sounds like ye in yes

예 s

ye		e
ㅖ	from	ㅔ

TRACK 16

ye
ㅖ

ㅇ	+	ye ㅖ	=	ye 예
g ㄱ	+	ye ㅖ	=	gye 계
r ㄹ	+	ye ㅖ	=	rye 례
s ㅅ	+	ye ㅖ	=	sye 셰
p ㅍ	+	ye ㅖ	=	pye 폐

ㅖ

ye mae
예매 reservation

gi gye
기계 machine

sye peo deu
셰퍼드 shepherd

Find the letters ‘consonant + ㅖ’ in the images below.

세계

계절

예산, 수혜자

REVIEW

Read and write the following words.

ya gu 야구	야구		
sya weo 샤워	샤워		
e seu pa nya 에스파냐	에스파냐		
yeo ja 여자	여자		
sheo teo 셔터	셔터		
myeo neu ri 며느리	며느리		
yo ri 요리	요리		
myo sa 묘사	묘사		
sho teu ke i keu 쇼트케이크	쇼트케이크		

yu ri 유리	유리		
gyu mo 규모	규모		
nyu seu 뉴스	뉴스		
yae gi 얘기	얘기		
syae do 섀도	섀도		
ha yae yo 하얘요	하얘요		
ye mae 예매	예매		
gi gye 기계	기계		
sye peo deu 셰퍼드	셰퍼드		

3 The "W" Group Vowels

There are certain vowels created by merging 'o[ㅗ]' or 'u[ㅜ]' to other existing vowels. The vowels are double vowels. Because these are double vowels, when pronouncing them think of the letter "w" and pronounce them as you would pronounce words that begin "w."

1. Vowels created by adding other vowels to ㅗ (o)

Combination		Example
ㅗ (o→w) +	ㅏ (a) = ㅘ (wa)	와 과 놔 봐 좌
	ㅐ (ae) = ㅙ (wae)	왜 괘 돼 쇄 홰
	ㅣ (i→e) = ㅚ (we)	외 괴 되 쇠 회

2. Vowels created by adding other vowels to ㅜ (u)

Combination		Example
ㅜ (u→w) +	ㅓ (eo) = ㅝ (weo)	워 궈 눠 둬 줘
	ㅔ (e) = ㅞ (we)	웨 궤 퉤 쉐 훼
	ㅣ (i) = ㅟ (wi)	위 귀 뒤 쉬 쥐

TRACK 17

wa
와

weo
워

wae
왜

we
웨

we
외

wi
위

ㅘ(와) sounds like wa in "why"

와 y

wa		o→w		a
ㅘ	=	ㅗ	+	ㅏ

TRACK 18

wa

ㅘ

		wa		
ㅇ	+	ㅘ	=	와 (wa)
ㄱ (g)	+	ㅘ (wa)	=	과 (gwa)
ㅂ (b)	+	ㅘ (wa)	=	봐 (bwa)
ㅈ (j)	+	ㅘ (wa)	=	좌 (jwa)
ㅎ (h)	+	ㅘ (wa)	=	화 (hwa)

ㅘ

gi wa
기와 roof tile

gwa ja
과자 snacks

hwa ga
화가 painter

ㅘ ㅘ ㅘ

Find the letters ‘consonant + ㅘ’ in the images below.

과일

와인

화천

ㅙ(왜) sounds like wae in "western"

왜stern

wae		o→w		ae
ㅙ	=	ㅗ	+	ㅐ

TRACK 19

wae ㅙ

ㅇ	+	wae ㅙ	=	wae 왜
g ㄱ	+	wae ㅙ	=	gwae 괘
d ㄷ	+	wae ㅙ	=	dwae 돼
s ㅅ	+	wae ㅙ	=	swae 쇄
h ㅎ	+	wae ㅙ	=	hwae 홰

ㅙ

wae
왜? why?

dwae ji
돼지 pig

pye swae
폐쇄 shutdown

ㅙ ㅙ ㅙ

Find the letters ‘consonant + ㅙ’ in the images below.

돼지

폐쇄

왜가리

ㅚ(외) sounds like we in "wedding"

외dding

we		o→w		i→e
ㅚ	=	ㅗ	+	ㅣ

TRACK 20

we
ㅚ

ㅇ	+	ㅚ (we)	=	외 (we)
ㄱ (g)	+	ㅚ (we)	=	괴 (gwe)
ㄷ (d)	+	ㅚ (we)	=	되 (dwe)
ㅅ (s)	+	ㅚ (we)	=	쇠 (swe)
ㅎ (h)	+	ㅚ (we)	=	회 (hwe)

ㅚ

we ga
외가 relative on the mother's side

hwe sa
회사 company

yu gwe
유괴 kidnap

① ② ③ ㅚ ㅚ ㅚ

Find the letters 'consonant + ㅚ' in the images below.

외국어

박람회

참외

ㅝ(워) sounds like weo in "worry"

워rry

weo		u→w		eo
ㅝ	=	ㅜ	+	ㅓ

TRACK 21

weo
ㅝ

ㅇ	+	ㅝ (weo)	=	워 (weo)
ㄴ (n)	+	ㅝ (weo)	=	눠 (nweo)
ㄷ (d)	+	ㅝ (weo)	=	둬 (dweo)
ㅁ (m)	+	ㅝ (weo)	=	뭐 (mweo)
ㅈ (j)	+	ㅝ (weo)	=	줘 (jweo)

ㅝ

sya weo
샤워 shower

mweo ye yo
뭐예요? what's it?

jweo yo
줘요 give me st.

ㅝ ㅝ ㅝ

Find the letters 'consonant + ㅝ' in the images below.

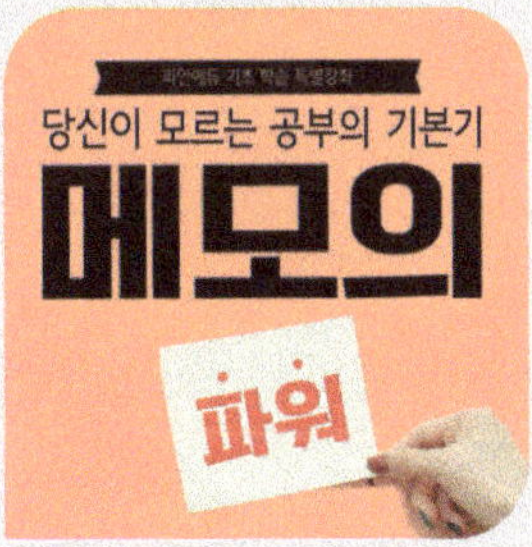

파워

워크숍

뭐?

ㅞ(웨) sounds like we in "weddingern"

웨ddingern

we ㅞ	=	u→w ㅜ	+	e ㅔ

TRACK 22

we
ㅞ

ㅇ	+	we ㅞ	=	we 웨
g ㄱ	+	we ㅞ	=	gwe 궤
d ㄷ	+	we ㅞ	=	dwe 뒈
s ㅅ	+	we ㅞ	=	swe 쉐
h ㅎ	+	we ㅞ	=	hwe 훼

ㅞ

we i teo
웨이터 waiter

gwe do
궤도 orbit

hwa hwe
화훼 floricultural

Find the letters 'consonant + ㅞ' in the images below.

스웨덴

웨딩

웨이스트

ㅟ(위) sounds like wi in "we"

위

wi		u→w		i
ㅟ	=	ㅜ	+	ㅣ

TRACK 23

wi

ㅟ

		wi		wi
ㅇ	+	ㅟ	=	위

g		wi		gwi
ㄱ	+	ㅟ	=	귀

d		wi		dwi
ㄷ	+	ㅟ	=	뒤

s		wi		swi
ㅅ	+	ㅟ	=	쉬

h		wi		hwi
ㅎ	+	ㅟ	=	휘

ㅟ

ga wi
가위 scissors

gwi
귀 ear

dwi
뒤 back

Find the letters ‘consonant + ㅟ’ in the images below.

귀향

뒤집기

위기

REVIEW

Read and write the following words.

gi wa 기와	기와		
gwa ja 과자	과자		
hwa ga 화가	화가		
wae 왜?	왜?		
dwae ji 돼지	돼지		
pye swae 폐쇄	폐쇄		
we ga 외가	외가		
hwe sa 회사	회사		
yu gwe 유괴	유괴		

sya weo 샤워	샤워		
mweo ye yo 뭐예요?	뭐예요?		
jweo yo 줘요	줘요		
we i teo 웨이터	웨이터		
gwe do 궤도	궤도		
hwa hwe 화훼	화훼		
ga wi 가위	가위		
gwi 귀	귀		
dwi 뒤	뒤		

4 The Diphthongs Vowel

eui		eu		i
ㅢ	=	ㅡ	+	ㅣ

TRACK 24

① When '의' is the first syllable of a words, it has the pronunciation of [의](eui)

② When '의' is not the first syllable of the word, it has the pronunciation of [이](i)

③ When it is used as a possessive marker, it is pronounced as [에](e)

ㅢ (eui)

ㅇ	+	ㅢ (eui)	=	의 (eui)
ㄴ (n)	+	ㅢ ((eu)i)	=	늬 (ni)
ㅎ (h)	+	ㅢ ((eu)i)	=	희 (hi)
ㄸ (dd)	+	ㅢ ((eu)i)	=	띄 (ddi)
ㅆ (ss)	+	ㅢ ((eu)i)	=	씌 (ssi)

ㅢ(의) sounds like eui in "ewww"

의 www

ㅢ

eui sa
의사 doctor

ju i
주의 caution

na e
나의 my

① ② ㅢ ㅢ ㅢ

Find the letters 'consonant + ㅢ' in the images below.

의료

꽃무늬

희망

REVIEW

eui sa 의사	의사		
ju i 주의	주의		
na e 나의	나의		

QUIZ

TRACK 25

Listen and write the words you hear.

1.

2.

3.

4.

5.

6.

7.

8.

9.

10.

What is your score?

/ 10

ANSWER

1. 아이 2. 어머니 3. 오리 4. 우주 5. 이모
6. 유리 7. 기계 8. 회사 9.가위 10. 주의

PART 2

Korean Consonants

1 The Composition of Korean Consonants

1. The Introduction of Korean Consonants

There is a sum total of fourteen basic consonants — some of which are used twice in a conjoined format to create five double consonants. In total, you get the following 19 consonants as per the table below.

ㄱ	ㄴ	ㄷ	ㄹ	ㅁ	ㅂ	ㅅ	ㅇ	ㅈ
ㅋ		ㅌ			ㅍ		ㅎ	ㅊ
ㄲ		ㄸ			ㅃ	ㅆ		ㅉ

The following is first five basic consonants.

g	n	m	s	
ㄱ	ㄴ	ㅁ	ㅅ	ㅇ

Adding a stroke to basic consonants such as ㄴ, ㅁ, ㅅ gives us normal-sound consonants such as ㄷ, ㅂ, ㅈ. Likewise, adding a stroke to the basic consonants such as ㄱ, ㄷ, ㅂ, ㅈ, ㅇ gives us the aspirated-sound consonant such as ㅋ, ㅌ, ㅍ, ㅊ, ㅎ.

Basic consonants and Applied consonants

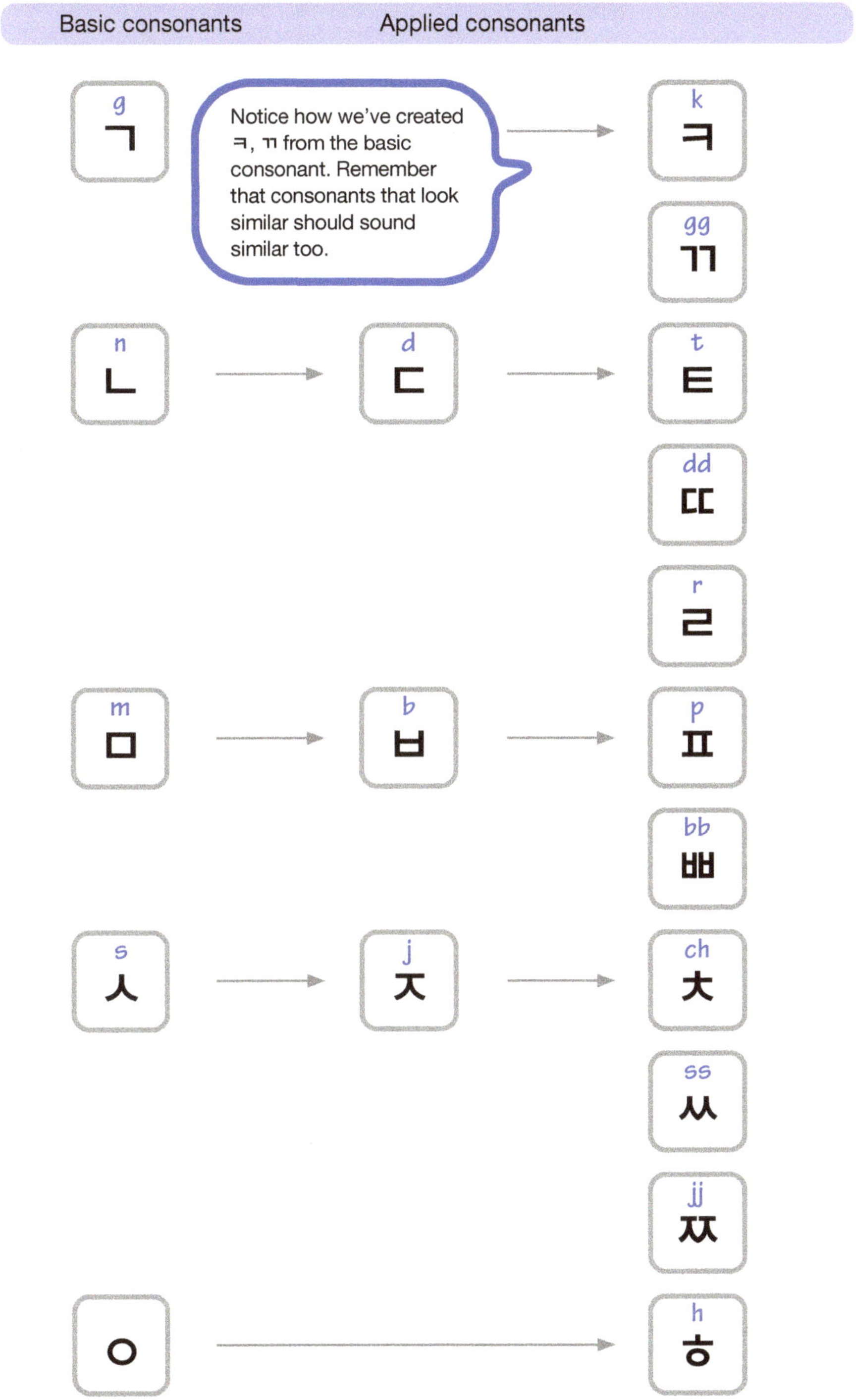

2. The Composition of Hangeul Syllables

There are three different variations to how we formulate syllables in Hangeul. First, there are stand-alone syllables with nothing but the vowel. Second, there are syllables which combine a consonant and a vowel. Third, there are syllables which put together a consonant and a vowel, joined by another consonant.

(A) Vowel Only

When a syllable is consisted of a single vowel, the empty consonant ' ㅇ ' is added to the left or above of the vowel to complete the sound.

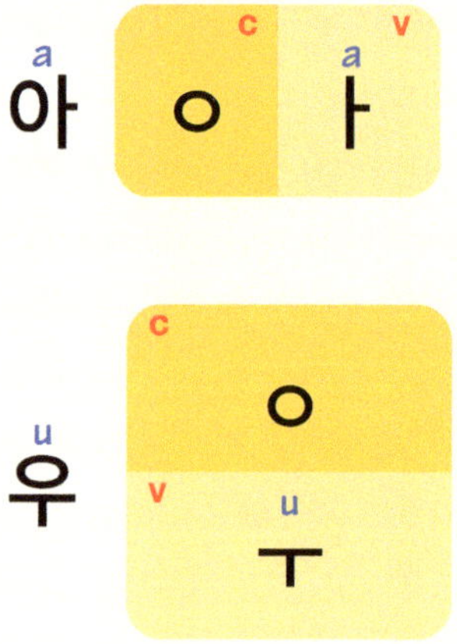

c : consonant
v : vowel

(B) Consonant + Vowel

For instance, you combine the consonant ㄴ[n] and vowel ㅏ[a] to create 나[na]. Likewise, you combine the consonant ㅁ[m] and vowel ㅜ[u] to create to 무[mu].

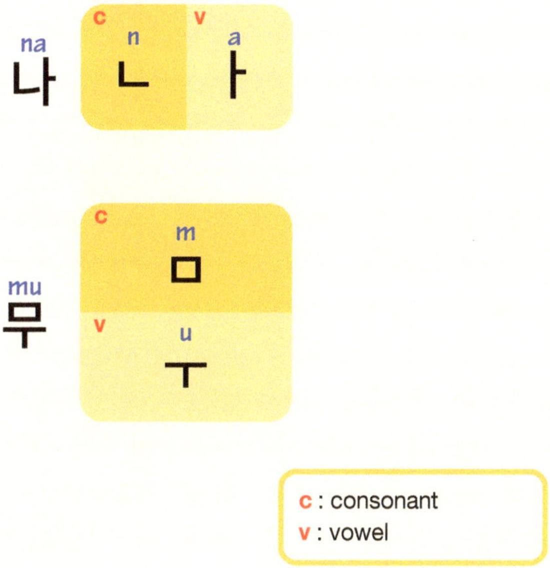

(C) Consonant + Vowel + Consonant

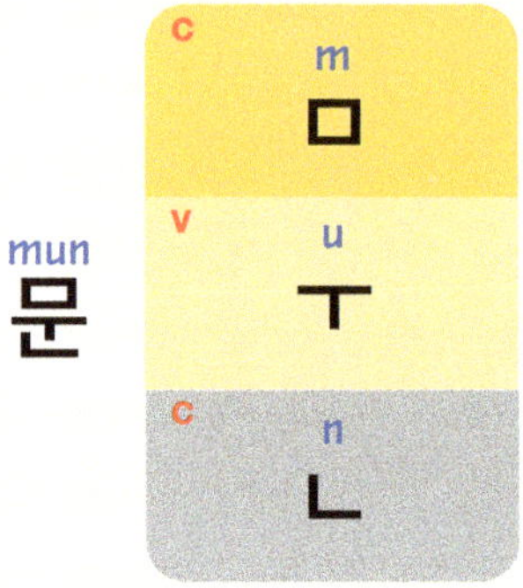

c : consonant
v : vowel

When a consonant is added underneath the consonant in a syllable, that consonant is called a 'batchim.'

Hangeul consonants are categorized into (1) Normal Sound (2) Aspirated Sound and (3) Tense Sound based on their pronunciation.

Normal sound	ㄱ	ㄴ	ㄷ	ㄹ	ㅁ	ㅂ	ㅅ	ㅇ	ㅈ
Aspirated sound	ㅋ		ㅌ			ㅍ		ㅎ	ㅊ
Tense sound	ㄲ		ㄸ			ㅃ	ㅆ		ㅉ

2 The Pronunciation of Consonants

1. Normal Sound

	a ㅏ	eo ㅓ	o ㅗ	u ㅜ	ae ㅐ	e ㅔ	eu ㅡ	i ㅣ
g ㄱ	ga 가	geo 거	go 고	gu 구	gae 개	ge 게	geu 그	gi 기
n ㄴ	na 나	neo 너	no 노	nu 누	nae 내	ne 네	neu 느	ni 니
d ㄷ	da 다	deo 더	do 도	du 두	dae 대	de 데	deu 드	di 디
r ㄹ	ra 라	reo 러	ro 로	ru 루	rae 래	re 레	reu 르	ri 리
m ㅁ	ma 마	meo 머	mo 모	mu 무	mae 매	me 메	meu 므	mi 미
b ㅂ	ba 바	beo 버	bo 보	bu 부	bae 배	be 베	beu 브	bi 비
s ㅅ	sa 사	seo 서	so 소	su 수	sae 새	se 세	seu 스	si 시
ㅇ	a 아	eo 어	o 오	u 우	ae 애	e 에	eu 으	i 이
j ㅈ	ja 자	jeo 저	jo 조	ju 주	jae 재	je 제	jeu 즈	ji 지

ㄱ (giyeok) is 'g' of gun.

g
ㄱ

ㄱ	+	a ㅏ	=	ga 가
ㄱ	+	eo ㅓ	=	geo 거
ㄱ	+	o ㅗ	=	go 고
ㄱ	+	u ㅜ	=	gu 구
ㄱ	+	eu ㅡ	=	geu 그
ㄱ	+	i ㅣ	=	gi 기
ㄱ	+	ae ㅐ	=	gae 개
ㄱ	+	e ㅔ	=	ge 게

ㄱ has the shape of a gun.
When you look at this alphabet, think of it as the letter "g" in gun.

TRACK 26

ㄱ

ga gu
가구 furniture

go gi
고기 meat

geu ri seu
그리스 Greece

Find the letters 'ㄱ + vowel' in the images below.

가족

군고구마, 겨울

그림

ㄴ (nieun) is 'n' of nose.

n
ㄴ

ㄴ	+	ㅏ (a)	=	나 (na)
ㄴ	+	ㅓ (eo)	=	너 (neo)
ㄴ	+	ㅗ (o)	=	노 (no)
ㄴ	+	ㅜ (u)	=	누 (nu)
ㄴ	+	ㅡ (eu)	=	느 (neu)
ㄴ	+	ㅣ (i)	=	니 (ni)
ㄴ	+	ㅐ (ae)	=	내 (nae)
ㄴ	+	ㅔ (e)	=	네 (ne)

ㄴ has the shape of a nose.
When you look at this alphabet, think of it as the letter "n" in nose.

TRACK 27

ㄴ

nu na	
누나	older sister

no rae	
노래	song

na ra	
나라	country

① ㄴ

ㄴ

ㄴ

ㄴ

Find the letters 'ㄴ + vowel' in the images below.

나

노래

바느질

ㄷ (digeut) is 'd' of door.

d
ㄷ

ㄷ	+	a ㅏ	=	da 다
ㄷ	+	eo ㅓ	=	deo 더
ㄷ	+	o ㅗ	=	do 도
ㄷ	+	u ㅜ	=	du 두
ㄷ	+	eu ㅡ	=	deu 드
ㄷ	+	i ㅣ	=	di 디
ㄷ	+	ae ㅐ	=	dae 대
ㄷ	+	e ㅔ	=	de 데

ㄷ has the shape of a door.
When you look at this alphabet, think of it as the letter "d" in door.

TRACK 28

ㄷ

da ri
다리 bridge/leg

deu ra i eo
드라이어
hairdryer

di ja i neo
디자이너
designer

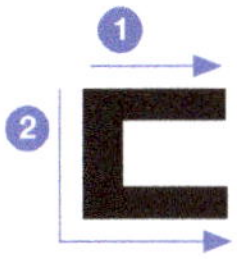

Find the letters 'ㄷ + vowel' in the images below.

다낭

더위

제주도, 그대로

ㄹ (rieul) is 'r' of ribbon.

r ㄹ	

ㄹ	+	a ㅏ	=	ra 라
ㄹ	+	eo ㅓ	=	reo 러
ㄹ	+	o ㅗ	=	ro 로
ㄹ	+	u ㅜ	=	ru 루
ㄹ	+	eu ㅡ	=	reu 르
ㄹ	+	i ㅣ	=	ri 리
ㄹ	+	ae ㅐ	=	rae 래
ㄹ	+	e ㅔ	=	re 레

ㄹ has the shape of a ribbon.
When you look at this alphabet, think of it as the letter "r" in ribbon.

TRACK 29

ㄹ

- ri deo — **리더** leader
- ra di o — **라디오** radio
- reu po — **르포** reportage

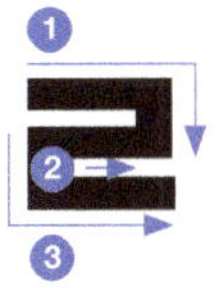

Find the letters 'ㄹ + vowel' in the images below.

요리

하루

모래

ㅁ (mieum) is 'm' of mouth.

m
ㅁ

					Vowel		Syllable
ㅁ	+	ㅏ	=	마	a		ma
ㅁ	+	ㅓ	=	머	eo		meo
ㅁ	+	ㅗ	=	모	o		mo
ㅁ	+	ㅜ	=	무	u		mu
ㅁ	+	ㅡ	=	므	eu		meu
ㅁ	+	ㅣ	=	미	i		mi
ㅁ	+	ㅐ	=	매	ae		mae
ㅁ	+	ㅔ	=	메	e		me

ㅁ has the shape of a mouth.
When you look at this alphabet, think of it as the letter "m" in mouth.

TRACK 30

ㅁ

mi ni
미니 mini

mo ja
모자 hat

meo ri
머리 head

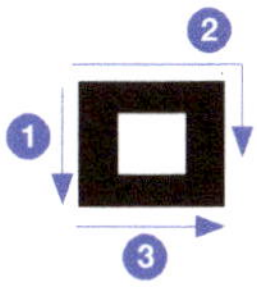

Find the letters 'ㅁ + vowel' in the images below.

메리 크리스마스

무료

매미

ㅂ (bieup) is 'b' of bucket.

ㅂ (b)

ㅂ	+	ㅏ (a)	=	바 (ba)
ㅂ	+	ㅓ (eo)	=	버 (beo)
ㅂ	+	ㅗ (o)	=	보 (bo)
ㅂ	+	ㅜ (u)	=	부 (bu)
ㅂ	+	ㅡ (eu)	=	브 (beu)
ㅂ	+	ㅣ (i)	=	비 (bi)
ㅂ	+	ㅐ (ae)	=	배 (bae)
ㅂ	+	ㅔ (e)	=	베 (be)

ㅅ has the shape of a sandwich.
When you look at this alphabet, think of it as the letter "s" in sandwich.

TRACK 32

ㅅ

seo bi seu	서비스	service
sa ja	사자	lion
ga su	가수	singer

ㅅ

ㅅ

ㅅ

ㅅ

Find the letters 'ㅅ + vowel' in the images below.

감사

서울

시간

ㅈ (jieut) is 'j' of jeans.

j
ㅈ

					vowel		syllable
ㅈ	+	ㅏ	a	=	자	ja	
ㅈ	+	ㅓ	eo	=	저	jeo	
ㅈ	+	ㅗ	o	=	조	jo	
ㅈ	+	ㅜ	u	=	주	ju	
ㅈ	+	ㅡ	eu	=	즈	jeu	
ㅈ	+	ㅣ	i	=	지	ji	
ㅈ	+	ㅐ	ae	=	재	jae	
ㅈ	+	ㅔ	e	=	제	je	

ㅈ has the shape of jeans.
When you look at this alphabet, think of it as the letter "j" in jeans.

TRACK 33

ㅈ

ju 주 seu 스 juce

ji 지 gu 구 earth

chi 치 jeu 즈 cheese

ㅈ

ㅈ

ㅈ

Find the letters '**ㅈ** + vowel' in the images below.

자랑, 자취

정지

주차금지

REVIEW

Read and write the following words.

ga gu 가구	가구		
go gi 고기	고기		
geu ri seu 그리스	그리스		
nu na 누나	누나		
no rae 노래	노래		
na ra 나라	나라		
da ri 다리	다리		
deu ra i eo 드라이어	드라이어		
di ja i neo 디자이너	디자이너		
ri deo 리더	리더		

ra di o 라디오	라디오		
reu po 르포	르포		
mi ni 미니	미니		
mo ja 모자	모자		
meo ri 머리	머리		
beo seu 버스	버스		
ba da 바다	바다		
bi ja 비자	비자		
seo bi seu 서비스	서비스		
sa ja 사자	사자		

ju seu 주스	주스		
ji gu 지구	지구		
chi jeu 치즈	치즈		

2. Aspirated sound

There are consonants created by adding a stroke or dot to the basic consonants 'ㄱ, ㄷ, ㅂ, ㅇ, ㅈ.' They are 'ㅋ, ㅌ, ㅍ, ㅎ, ㅊ' and are called aspirated consonants. When pronouncing the aspirated consonants, please refrain from creating vibration in the vocal cord.

Aspirated Consonants: Names and Usage

TRACK 34

Consonants	Name	Pronunciation Tips	Examples
ㅋ	ki euk 키읔	Aspirated k as in kill	ka ki ku ke ko 카 키 쿠 케 코 카드 card 쿠키 cookie
ㅌ	ti eut 티읕	Aspirated t in talk	ta ti tu te to 타 티 투 테 토 타조 ostrich 도토리 acorn
ㅍ	pi eup 피읖	Aspirated p as in power	pa pi pu pe po 파 피 푸 페 포 피아노 piano 아파트 apartment
ㅎ	hi eut 히읗	Aspirated h as in how	ha hi hu he ho 하 히 후 헤 호 하나 one 오후 afternoon
ㅊ	chi eut 치읓	Aspirated ch as in change	cha chi chu che cho 차 치 추 체 초 치마 skirt 고추 chili pepper

ㅋ (kieuk) is 'k' of key.

k ㅋ	ㅋ	+	a ㅏ	=	ka 카
	ㅋ	+	eo ㅓ	=	keo 커
	ㅋ	+	o ㅗ	=	ko 코
	ㅋ	+	u ㅜ	=	ku 쿠
	ㅋ	+	eu ㅡ	=	keu 크
	ㅋ	+	i ㅣ	=	ki 키
	ㅋ	+	ae ㅐ	=	kae 캐
	ㅋ	+	e ㅔ	=	ke 케

ㅋ has the shape of a key.
When you look at this alphabet, think of it as the letter "k" in key.

TRACK 35

ㅋ

ku ki	쿠키	cookie
ka ka o	카카오	cacao
ko ko a	코코아	cocoa

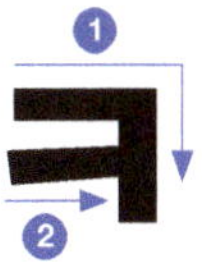

Find the letters 'ㅋ + vowel' in the images below.

스케치북

쿠키, 케이크, 마카롱

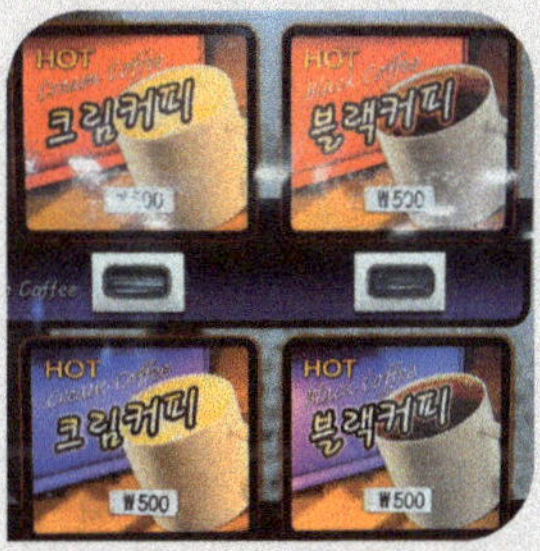

커피

ㅌ (tieut) is 't' of track.

t
ㅌ

ㅌ	+	a ㅏ	=	ta 타
ㅌ	+	eo ㅓ	=	teo 터
ㅌ	+	o ㅗ	=	to 토
ㅌ	+	u ㅜ	=	tu 투
ㅌ	+	eu ㅡ	=	teu 트
ㅌ	+	i ㅣ	=	ti 티
ㅌ	+	ae ㅐ	=	tae 태
ㅌ	+	e ㅔ	=	te 테

ㅌ has the shape of a track.
When you look at this alphabet, think of it as the letter “t” in track.

TRACK 36

ㅌ

to	seu	teu	
토	스	트	toast

gi	ta	
기	타	guitar

te	ni	seu	
테	니	스	tennis

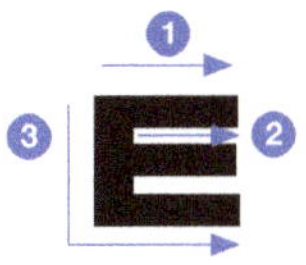

ㅌ

ㅌ

ㅌ

Find the letters ‘ㅌ + vowel’ in the images below.

토마토

투자

다이어트

ㅍ (pieup) is 'p' of piano.

p
ㅍ

ㅍ	+	a ㅏ	=	pa 파
ㅍ	+	eo ㅓ	=	peo 퍼
ㅍ	+	o ㅗ	=	po 포
ㅍ	+	u ㅜ	=	pu 푸
ㅍ	+	eu ㅡ	=	peu 프
ㅍ	+	i ㅣ	=	pi 피
ㅍ	+	ae ㅐ	=	pae 패
ㅍ	+	e ㅔ	=	pe 페

ㅍ has the shape of a piano.
When you look at this alphabet, think of it as the letter "p" in piano.

TRACK 37

ㅍ

pi a no	피아노	piano
pa ri	파리	Paris
na i peu	나이프	knife

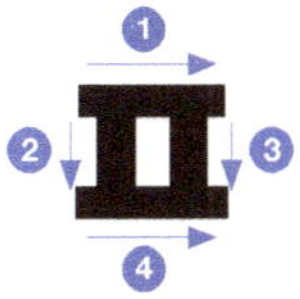

Find the letters '**ㅍ** + vowel' in the images below.

파티

푸시

레시피

ㅎ (hieut) is 'h' of hat.

h ㅎ	ㅎ	+	a ㅏ	=	ha 하
	ㅎ	+	eo ㅓ	=	heo 허
	ㅎ	+	o ㅗ	=	ho 호
	ㅎ	+	u ㅜ	=	hu 후
	ㅎ	+	eu ㅡ	=	heu 흐
	ㅎ	+	i ㅣ	=	hi 히
	ㅎ	+	ae ㅐ	=	hae 해
	ㅎ	+	e ㅔ	=	he 헤

ㅎ has the shape of a hat.
When you look at this alphabet, think of it as the letter "h" in hat.

▶ TRACK 38

ㅎ

hi teo
히터 heater

ha ma
하마 hippo

heo ri
허리 waist

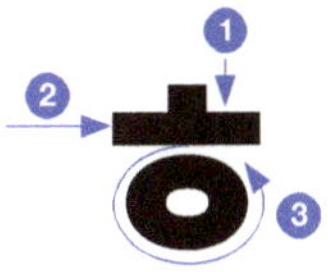

ㅎ ㅎ ㅎ

Find the letters 'ㅎ + vowel' in the images below.

하나

비보호

후기

ㅊ (chieut) is 'ch' of cha-cha-cha.

ch
ㅊ

ㅊ	+	ㅏ (a)	=	차 (cha)
ㅊ	+	ㅓ (eo)	=	처 (cheo)
ㅊ	+	ㅗ (o)	=	초 (cho)
ㅊ	+	ㅜ (u)	=	추 (chu)
ㅊ	+	ㅡ (eu)	=	츠 (cheu)
ㅊ	+	ㅣ (i)	=	치 (chi)
ㅊ	+	ㅐ (ae)	=	채 (chae)
ㅊ	+	ㅔ (e)	=	체 (che)

ㅊ has the shape of cha-cha-cha.
When you look at this alphabet, think of it as the letter "ch" in cha-cha-cha.

TRACK 39

ㅊ

chi ta
치타 cheetah

cho
초 candle

seu po cheu
스포츠 sports

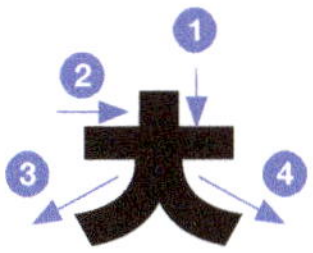

Find the letters '**ㅊ** + vowel' in the images below.

녹차

채소

추천

REVIEW

Read and write the following words.

ku ki 쿠키	쿠키		
ka ka o 카카오	카카오		
to seu teu 토스트	토스트		
gi ta 기타	기타		
pi a no 피아노	피아노		
pa ri 파리	파리		
hi teo 히터	히터		
heo ri 허리	허리		
chi ta 치타	치타		
seu po cheu 스포츠	스포츠		

3. Tense sound

There are consonants created by conjoining two of the same consonants 'ㄱ, ㄷ, ㅂ, ㅅ, ㅈ' in order to create a set of tense-sounding consonants such as 'ㄲ, ㄸ, ㅃ, ㅆ, ㅉ' respectively. Tense sounds strain the articulators and when pronouncing these consonants, one must beware not to exhale while making the sound.

Tense Consonants: Names and Usage

TRACK 40

Consonants	Name	Pronunciation Tips	Examples
ㄲ	쌍기역 (ssang gi yeok)	**Tense g as in skill**	까 (gga) 끼 (ggi) 꾸 (ggu) 께 (gge) 꼬 (ggo) 꼬리 tail 아까 while ago
ㄸ	쌍디귿 (ssang di geut)	**Tense d as in steel**	따 (dda) 띠 (ddi) 뚜 (ddu) 떼 (dde) 또 (ddo) 따로 separately 이따가 later
ㅃ	쌍비읍 (ssang bi eup)	**Tense b as in speech**	빠 (bba) 삐 (bbi) 뿌 (bbu) 빼 (bbe) 뽀 (bbo) 빠르다 fast 뽀뽀 kiss
ㅆ	쌍시옷 (ssang si ot)	**Tense s as in sit**	싸 (ssa) 씨 (ssi) 쑤 (ssu) 쎄 (sse) 쏘 (sso) 싸다 cheap 아가씨 ladies
ㅉ	쌍지읒 (ssang ji eut)	**Tense j as in judge**	짜 (jja) 찌 (jji) 쭈 (jju) 쩨 (jje) 쪼 (jjo) 짜다 salty 가짜 fake

ㄲ (ssang giyeok) is tense g as in skill.

gg

ㄲ

ㄲ	+	ㅏ (a)	=	까 (gga)
ㄲ	+	ㅓ (eo)	=	꺼 (ggeo)
ㄲ	+	ㅗ (o)	=	꼬 (ggo)
ㄲ	+	ㅜ (u)	=	꾸 (ggu)
ㄲ	+	ㅡ (eu)	=	끄 (ggeu)
ㄲ	+	ㅣ (i)	=	끼 (ggi)
ㄲ	+	ㅐ (ae)	=	깨 (ggae)
ㄲ	+	ㅔ (e)	=	께 (gge)

TRACK 41

ㄲ

gga *chi*
까치 magpie

ggo *ma*
꼬마 kid

ggae
깨 sesame

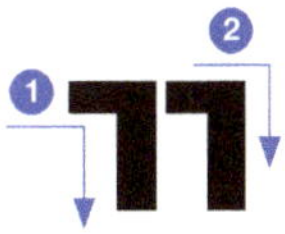

Find the letters '**ㄲ** + vowel' in the images below.

시킬까

꾸안꾸

꼬막

ㄸ (ssang digeut) is tense d as in steel.

dd
ㄸ

ㄸ	+	a ㅏ	=	dda 따
ㄸ	+	eo ㅓ	=	ddeo 떠
ㄸ	+	o ㅗ	=	ddo 또
ㄸ	+	u ㅜ	=	ddu 뚜
ㄸ	+	eu ㅡ	=	ddeu 뜨
ㄸ	+	i ㅣ	=	ddi 띠
ㄸ	+	ae ㅐ	=	ddae 때
ㄸ	+	e ㅔ	=	dde 떼

TRACK 42

ㄸ

heo ri ddi
허리띠 belt

ddo
또 again

ddae ddae ro
때때로 sometimes

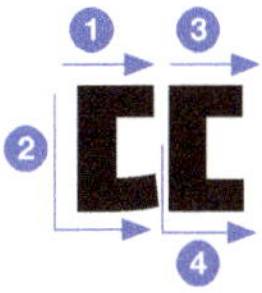

Find the letters 'ㄸ + vowel' in the images below.

떠나자, 따라

따뜻한

뛰지

ㅃ (ssang bieup) is tense b as in speech.

bb
ㅃ

ㅃ	+	a ㅏ	=	bba 빠
ㅃ	+	eo ㅓ	=	bbeo 뻐
ㅃ	+	o ㅗ	=	bbo 뽀
ㅃ	+	u ㅜ	=	bbu 뿌
ㅃ	+	eu ㅡ	=	bbeu 쁘
ㅃ	+	i ㅣ	=	bbi 삐
ㅃ	+	ae ㅐ	=	bbae 빼
ㅃ	+	e ㅔ	=	bbe 뻬

TRACK 43

ㅃ

bbo bbo
뽀뽀 kiss

bbu ri
뿌리 root

o bba
오빠 older brother

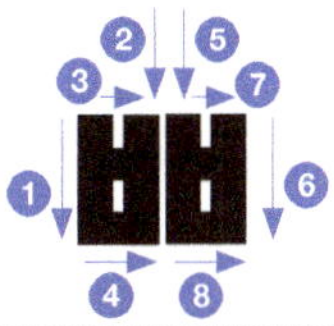

Find the letters '**ㅃ** + vowel' in the images below.

빠른

빼빼로

뿌리

ㅆ (ssang siot) is tense s as in sit.

ss
ㅆ

ㅆ	+	a	ㅏ	=	ssa 싸
ㅆ	+	eo	ㅓ	=	sseo 써
ㅆ	+	o	ㅗ	=	sso 쏘
ㅆ	+	u	ㅜ	=	ssu 쑤
ㅆ	+	eu	ㅡ	=	sseu 쓰
ㅆ	+	i	ㅣ	=	ssi 씨
ㅆ	+	ae	ㅐ	=	ssae 쌔
ㅆ	+	e	ㅔ	=	sse 쎄

TRACK 44

ㅆ

bi ssa yo
비 싸 요 expensive

sseu da
쓰 다 write

ssi
씨 seed

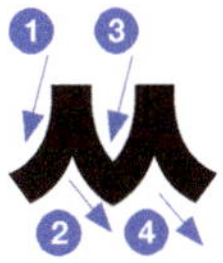

Find the letters 'ㅆ + vowel' in the images below.

싸움

쏘가리

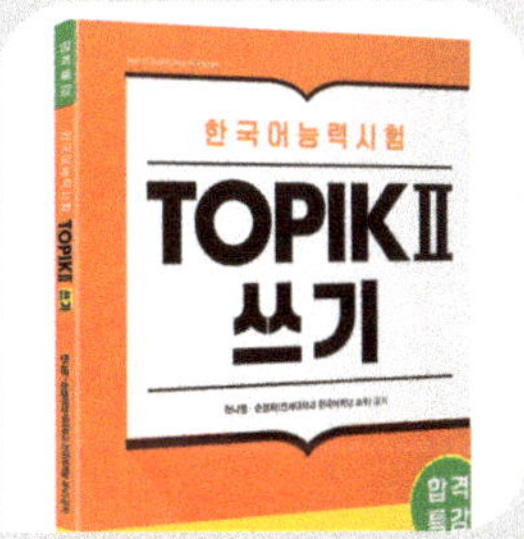

쓰기

ㅉ (ssang jieut) is tense j as in judge.

jj
ㅉ

ㅉ	+	ㅏ (a)	=	짜 (jja)
ㅉ	+	ㅓ (eo)	=	쩌 (jjeo)
ㅉ	+	ㅗ (o)	=	쪼 (jjo)
ㅉ	+	ㅜ (u)	=	쭈 (jju)
ㅉ	+	ㅡ (eu)	=	쯔 (jjeu)
ㅉ	+	ㅣ (i)	=	찌 (jji)
ㅉ	+	ㅐ (ae)	=	째 (jjae)
ㅉ	+	ㅔ (e)	=	쩨 (jje)

TRACK 45

ㅉ

jji gae
찌 개 Korean style stew

jja da
짜 다 salty

jjo gae da
쪼 개 다 spilt

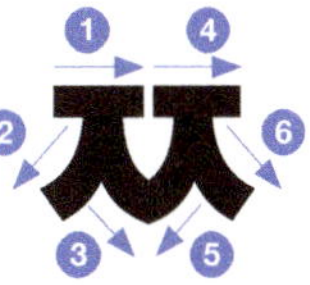

ㅉ

ㅉ

ㅉ

Find the letters '**ㅉ** + vowel' in the images below.

짜다

쪼개기

찌개

REVIEW

Read and write the following words.

gga chi 까치	까치		
ggae 깨	깨		
heo ri ddi 허리띠	허리띠		
ddo 또	또		
bbu ri 뿌리	뿌리		
o bba 오빠	오빠		
sseu da 쓰다	쓰다		
ssi 씨	씨		
jji gae 찌개	찌개		
jja da 짜다	짜다		

4. 'Batchim', final consonant ①

In Korean, a vowel and a consonant are combined to form one character, and you can further add a final consonant called **'batchim'** under the set. The batchim is an important part of Korean pronunciation because it often determines a change in the way words are pronounced.

다, 가 – no batchim
달, 갑 – ㄹ and ㅂ are the batchim
닭, 값 – ㄺ and ㅄ are the double batchim

Next, let's learn about the types of batchim and their pronunciation.

There are 16 consonants that are used as batchim, but there are only 7 kinds (ㄱ, ㄴ, ㄷ, ㄹ, ㅁ, ㅂ, ㅇ) of pronunciation.

In other words, there are different characters that have the same pronunciation.

List of batchim

ㄱ	ㄴ	ㄷ	ㄹ	ㅁ	ㅂ	ㅅ	ㅇ	ㅈ
ㅊ	ㅋ	ㅌ	ㅍ	ㅎ	ㄲ	ㅆ		

TRACK 46

Final Consonant	How to read	Examples
ㄱ ㅋ ㄲ	k ㄱ	chaek 책(book), bu eok 부엌[부억](kitchen), bak 밖[박](outside)
ㄴ	n ㄴ	don 돈(money), san 산(mountain)
ㄷ ㅅ ㅈ ㅊ ㅌ ㅎ ㅆ	t ㄷ	sut ga rak 숟가락(spoon), ot 옷[옫](cloth), nat 낮[낟](noon), ggot 꽃[꼳](flower), ggeut 끝[끋](end), hi eut 히읗[히읃](the name of ㅎ), it dda 있다[읻따](being)
ㄹ	l ㄹ	dal 달(moon), mul 물(water)
ㅁ	m ㅁ	mom 몸(body), bom 봄(spring)
ㅂ ㅍ	p ㅂ	ip 입(mouth), ap 앞(front)
ㅇ	ng ㅇ	gang 강(river), gong 공(ball)

Resyllabification and Pronunciations of Korean Consonants

Suppose the previous syllable ends in a consonant in the final position, and the next syllable begins with the letter ㅇ. In that case, the consonant sound gets moved to the beginning of the following syllable.

TRACK 47

단어 → da neo [다너]

음악 → eu mak [으막]

밥이 → ba bi [바비]

먹어요 → meo geo yo [머거요]

ㄱ(ㅋ, ㄲ)

First, ㄱ, ㅋ and ㄲ make the **k** sound. These three letters look similar and can sound similar. Keep your tongue still and your throat should feel a little choked. Let's practice by reading **악**, **앜**, **앆**.

▶ TRACK 48

Consonant		Final Consonant	
ㄱ (g)	가 (ga)	[ㄱ] k	각[각] ga k
ㅋ (k)	카 (ka)		갘[각] ga k
ㄲ (gg)	까 (gga)		갂[각] ga k

ㄱ ㅋ ㄲ

- 미국 (mi gu k) America
- 부엌 (bu eo k) kitchen
- 밖 (ba k) outside

Find the letters batchim [ㄱ] in the images below.

축제

팥죽, 호박죽

대한민국

ㄴ

Secondly, **ㄴ** makes the **n** sound. Your tongue should touch the back of your upper teeth. This "n" sound is the correct pronunciation of **ㄴ** batchim. Or, try slightly biting your tongue with your front teeth and say "Nnn." Let's practice this time with **안**.

TRACK 49

Consonant		Final Consonant	
ㄴ (n)	나 (na)	n [ㄴ]	난[난] (na n)

ㄴ

산 (sa n) mountain

돈 (do n) money

Find the letters batchim [ㄴ] in the images below.

안내

치킨

친구

ㄷ(ㅅ, ㅈ, ㅊ, ㅌ, ㅎ, ㅆ)

Consonant		Final Consonant	
d ㄷ	da 다	[ㄷ] t	닫[닫] da t
s ㅅ	sa 사		삿[삳] sa t
j ㅈ	ja 자		잦[잗] ja t
ch ㅊ	cha 차		찿[찯] cha t
t ㅌ	ta 타		탙[탇] ta t
h ㅎ	ha 하		핳[핟] ha t
ss ㅆ	ssa 싸		쌌[싿] ssa t

ㄷ, ㅅ, ㅈ, ㅊ, ㅌ, ㅎ, ㅆ all make the **t** sound. The tongue should touch the back of the upper teeth. Be aware that all these 7 kinds of batchim are pronounced the same with the "t" sound. Let's try practicing **앋, 앗, 앚, 앛, 앝, 앟, 았**. The batchims are different but they all have the same pronunciation.

TRACK 50

ㄷ ㅅ ㅈ ㅊ ㅌ ㅎ ㅆ		
	곧 go t	soon
	옷 o t	clothes
	낮 na t	noon
	빛 bi t	light
	밭 ba t	field

Find the letters batchim [ㄷ] in the images below.

닫아

스팟

끝

ㄹ

Fourthly, ㄹ makes the l sound. The tongue touches the upper teeth or the ceiling of the mouth. When you pronounce Lu, your tongue should touch the back of the ceiling of your mouth, right? This is the correct pronunciation of ㄹ. Let's practice by saying 알.

TRACK 51

Consonant		Final Consonant	
r ㄹ	ra 라	[ㄹ] l	랄[랄] ra l

ㄹ

달 da l — moon

날 na l — day

Find the letters batchim [ㄹ] in the images below.

마늘

한달, 살기

울릉도

ㅁ

The fifth is **ㅁ** with the **m** sound. It's an easy pronunciation which you just need to close your mouth. Let's practice by saying **암**.

TRACK 52

Consonant		Final Consonant	
m ㅁ	ma 마	[ㅁ] m	맘[맘] ma m

몸 mo m body

밤 ba m night

Find the letters batchim [ㅁ] in the images below.

봄

군밤

캠핑

ㅂ(ㅍ)

ㅂ and ㅍ have the **p** sound. Again, you just need to close your mouth. These also have the same pronunciation although the batchims are different. Let's practice with **압**, **앞**.

TRACK 53

Consonant		Final Consonant	
b **ㅂ**	ba **바**	[ㅂ] **p**	밥[밥] ba p
p **ㅍ**	pa **파**		팝[팝] pa p

ㅂ ㅍ

- **밥** ba p — meal
- **앞** a p — front

Find the letters batchim [ㅂ] in the images below.

국밥

집값, 매입

농업인

ㅇ

ㅇ batchim makes the **ng** sound. When you pronounce this batchim, make a cave inside your mouth and don't move your tongue. Let's practice by saying **앙**.

▶ TRACK 54

Consonant		Final Consonant	
ㅇ	아 (a)	[ㅇ] **ng**	앙[앙] (a ng)

ㅇ

강 (ga ng) river

공 (go ng) ball

Find the letters batchim [ㅇ] in the images below.

운동, 건강

붕어빵

행복, 세상

5. 'Batchim', final consonant ② double batchim

The next is the double batchim. There are 11 double batchim in total. Some batchim are made of two consonants and they are called double batchim.

List of double batchim

Double batchim	Sound
ㄳ	k ㄱ
ㄺ	k ㄱ
ㄵ	n ㄴ
ㄶ	n ㄴ
ㄼ	l ㄹ
ㅀ	l ㄹ
ㄻ	m ㅁ
ㅄ	p ㅂ

Other double batchims, such as ㄽ, ㄾ, and ㄿ, are used less frequently and have therefore been omitted from this book.

TRACK 55

Final Consonant	How to read	Example
ㄳ	k ㄱ	sak 삯[삭] (wage)
ㄵ ㄶ	n ㄴ	an dda 앉다[안따] (sit) man ta 많다[만타] (many)
ㄺ*	k ㄱ	dak 닭[닥] (chicken)
ㄼ ㅀ	l ㄹ	yeo deol 여덟[여덜] (eight) il ta 잃다 [일타] (lose)
ㄻ*	m ㅁ	sam 삶[삼] (life)
ㅄ	p ㅂ	gap 값[갑] (price)

* ㄺ and ㄻ are pronounced with the right consonant.

(A) Read the left batchim

ㄳ [ㄱ] (k)	ㄵ [ㄴ] (n)
삯 sa k	앉다 a n dda
wage	sit

ㄶ [ㄴ] (n)	ㅄ [ㅂ] (p)
많다 ma n ta	값 ga p
many	price

ㄼ [ㄹ] (l)	ㅀ [ㄹ] (l)
여덟 yeo deo l	잃다 i l ta
eight	lose

(B) Read the right batchim

ㄺ [ㄱ] (k)	ㄻ [ㅁ] (m)
닭 da k	삶 sa m
chicken	life

* The letters ㄺ and ㄻ are read on the right.

TRACK 56

Find the letters **double batchim** in the images below.

끓여서

닭

많이

In some cases, when the next syllable begins with a vowel, the sound of the latter of the consonants simply gets transferred to the following syllable.

TRACK 57

값 → [갑] (gap)

값이 → [갑시] (gap si)

닭 → [닥] (dak)

닭이 → [달기] (dal gi)

삶 → [삼] (sam)

삶이 → [살미] (sal mi)

REVIEW

Read and write the following words.

mi guk 미국	미국		
bu eok 부엌	부엌		
bak 밖	밖		
san 산	산		
don 돈	돈		
got 곧	곧		
ot 옷	옷		
nat 낮	낮		
bit 빛	빛		
bat 밭	밭		

dal 달	달		
nal 날	날		
mom 몸	몸		
bam 밤	밤		
bap 밥	밥		
ap 앞	앞		
gang 강	강		
gong 공	공		

sak 삯	삯		
an dda 앉다	앉다		
man ta 많다	많다		
dak 닭	닭		
yeo deol 여덟	여덟		
il ta 잃다	잃다		
sam 삶	삶		
gap 값	값		

APPENDIX

1. Various fonts in Hangeul

가 나 다 라 마 바 사

아 자 차 카 타 파 하

가 나 다 라 마 바 사

아 자 차 카 타 파 하

가 나 다 라 마 바 사

아 자 차 카 타 파 하

가 나 다 라 마 바 사

아 자 차 카 타 파 하

2. Korean basic expression

TRACK 58

an-nyeong

안녕!

안녕!

Hi!

TRACK 59

an-nyeong-ha-se-yo

안녕하세요.

안녕하세요.

Hello.

TRACK 60

ban-ga-weo-yo

반가워요.

반가워요.

Nice to meet you.

TRACK 61

cheo-eum bwep-get-sseum-ni-da

처음 뵙겠습니다.

처음 뵙겠습니다.

It's a pleasure to meet you.

TRACK 62

o-raen-ma-ni-e-yo

오랜만이에요.

오랜만이에요.

Long time no see.

TRACK 63

jal ji-naet-sseo-yo

잘 지냈어요?

잘 지냈어요?

Have you been well?

TRACK 64

an-nyeong-hi gye-se-yo
안녕히 계세요.

안녕히 계세요.

Bye. (The one sending sb off)

TRACK 65

an-nyeong-hi ga-se-yo
안녕히 가세요.

안녕히 가세요.

Bye. (The one leaving sb)

TRACK 66

ne
네.

네.

Yes.

TRACK 67

a-ni-yo
아니요.

아니요.

No.

TRACK 68

go-ma-weo-yo

고마워요.

고마워요.

Thank you.

TRACK 69

gam-sa-ham-ni-da

감사합니다.

감사합니다.

Thank you.

TRACK 70

cheon-ma-ne-yo

천만에요.

천만에요.

You're welcome.

TRACK 71

sil-le-ham-ni-da

실례합니다.

실례합니다.

Excuse me.

TRACK 72

mi-an-hae-yo

미안해요.

미안해요.

Sorry.

TRACK 73

gwaen-cha-na-yo

괜찮아요.

괜찮아요.

It's okay.

il 일 1	일		i 이 2	이	
sam 삼 3	삼		sa 사 4	사	
o 오 5	오		yuk 육 6	육	
chil 칠 7	칠		pal 팔 8	팔	
gu 구 9	구		sip 십 10	십	

ha-na 하나 1	하나		dul 둘 2	둘	
set 셋 3	셋		net 넷 4	넷	
da-seot 다섯 5	다섯		yeo-seot 여섯 6	여섯	
il-gop 일곱 7	일곱		yeo-deol 여덟 8	여덟	
a-hop 아홉 9	아홉		yeol 열 10	열	

www.ingramcontent.com/pod-product-compliance
Lightning Source LLC
LaVergne TN
LVHW051038070526
838201LV00066B/4853
* 9 7 9 8 3 4 9 2 7 8 7 3 0 *